BRITISH WOMEN'S WORK DURING THE GREAT WAR

with a list of women who died on war service

The Naval & Military Press Ltd

in association with

The Imperial War Museum
Department of Printed Books

Published jointly by
The Naval & Military Press Ltd
Unit 10 Ridgewood Industrial Park,
Uckfield, East Sussex,
TN22 5QE England
Tel: +44 (0) 1825 749494
Fax: +44 (0) 1825 765701
www.naval–military-press.com
www.military-genealogy.com
www.militarymaproom.com

and

The Imperial War Museum, London
Department of Printed Books
www.iwm.org.uk

BRITISH WOMEN'S WORK DURING THE GREAT WAR 1914-1918.

At the outbreak of war, in August 1914, Great
Britain, with her powerful Navy, and small standing Army,
immediately threw all her resources into the conflict,
realising that the struggle would be a grim and
possibly prolonged one. One of the first problems which
arose was the flight of the Belgian refugees into England
from their own devastated country, and at once, women
stepped into the breach. Hostels were opened; Clearing
Homes established, and before long, considerable
machinery was set up for dealing adequately with the
situation.

The Nursing Services came at once into action.
Queen Alexandra's Imperial Military Nursing Service,
with a personnel of 300 and a large reserve staff
was called up, and six parties went to Belgium and
France on August 20th. 1914. The Territorial Force
Nursing Service, then eight years old, was mobilised
on August 5th, and within ten days, the whole personnel
of some 3,000 women was engaged, and 23 Territorial
General Hospitals in Great Britain were ready to receive the
wounded. The Naval Nurses, about 70 strong, with a
reserve staff were also available, and the whole of
the resources of the British Red Cross Organisation,
and that of the Order of St. John of Jerusalem, were

taken over by the War Office and Admiralty. Details of their work will be given later in this article.

Before many months were over, it was realised that the position of Great Britain would differ from that of any of the other countries involved in the war, in that she would be required to provide men, munitions, nursing services, equipment and transport, not on one Front only, but nearly all over the world. In Serbia, East Africa, Egypt, Mesopotamia, Gallipoli, Greece, Italy and India, as well as on the whole of the Western Front her men, her ships, her nurses, her ambulances, all were thrown into the fight, and as time went on, it became more and more evident that women as well as men would be needed to maintain all the essential services at home, to release men for the fighting line.

The Dominions, coming at once to the aid of the Allied Forces, had their own nurses, approximately 500 of whom served in France or in other theatres of War. Lady Minto's Indian Nursing Service served in India and Mesopotamia, and in hospital ships between India and the Persian Gulf.

Taking one example only, to show how magnificently women took their share of the burden, it may be mentioned that in August 1914 there were three National Munition Workshops in Great Britain. Before 1918, there were 100, and the Government also controlled over 5,000 establishments, through the Ministry of Munitions, which were concerned with supplies of various kinds. This was only made possible by the work of the women, and between 800,000 and 1,000,000 women worked in these establishments during the War.

In every department of the national life, women came forward and did men's work, from acting as bus-conductors to felling timber; they poured out from their homes all over the country - many who had never done any specialised work before - into the Government

offices, into the Banks, the Canteens, into every
kind of activity, with one idea only in their
minds - that of winning the war for the Allies.
It is impossible to estimate precisely the
effect of the women's attitude upon the final
result, but there can be no doubt that the brave
and determined outlook of the women at home and
abroad helped to support and sustain the fighting
units through the whole of that terrible struggle,
and spurred them on to victory.

When war broke out, women were fighting
for full recognition as citizens. They
abandoned that fight immediately they saw the danger
threatening their country, and the services they
rendered during those four years made it impossible any
longer to deny them the rights for which they had
pleaded. They had proved themselves worthy to stand side
by side with their men in peace, as they had done so
ungrudgingly in war.

This brief history of the work of British women
during the years 1914-1918 is necessarily incomplete,
since much of the work done was voluntary, and no
statistics are available, but it is a fairly comprehensive
survey of the many activities for which women were definitely
enrolled, and the total number cannot fall far short of
3,000,000. It has been divided, for convenience, into
three parts:-

1. The Nursing Services.   (Hospitals; women doctors;
                                 Voluntary Aid Detachments;
                                 Hospital Supplies; Ambulances;
                                 Drivers etc.)

2. Essential Home Services.   (Munitions; Canteens and Hostels;
                                 Land Army; Women Police; Transport
                                 Bus Conductors; Civil Service and
                                 Interpreters; Forage and Timber
                                 Corps; Refugees Committees; Concert
                                 Parties, etc.)

3. Navy, Army & Air Force.   (Queen Mary's Army Auxiliary Corps;
                                 Women's Royal Naval Service;
                                 Women's Royal Air Force; Women's
                                 Forage Corps.)

1.   THE NURSING SERVICES.

As has been stated, the existing official organisations were at once called up on the outbreak of war. Those 300 nurses and 800 Reserve staff in Queen Alexandra's Imperial Military Nursing Service were promptly drafted out to various Fronts, and during the war, 10,400 passed through the Service. Of these, 920 served on hospital ships, and over 6,000 in theatres of war. Many died on active service, and some were drowned or killed by enemy action. In addition to these 8,000 nurses passed through the Territorial Force Nursing Service, and 10,000 Voluntary Aid Detachment and other partly-trained nurses were attached to Imperial Units , making a total of over 28,000. Of the trained nurses, 159 died on service ; 141 members of V.A.D's of whom 29 nurses and 16 V.A.D members were killed or drowned.

Throughout the war, they showed complete indifference to danger, and operations were conducted under fire, and in face of every kind of difficulty. In the hospitals at home, they worked untiringly, and their record is one of unselfish and devoted service.

In England, hospitals of all kinds, both official and private, were staffed by the Red Cross Society, and the Order of St. John of Jerusalem. The total number of V.A.D's, whole and part time workers, was 80,000. Of these, 15,000 were enrolled for non-nursing duties, such as cooking and cleaning, and many of them drove ambulances in France and elsewhere, as did the women of the First-Aid/Nursing Yeomanry. A special Corps, The Almeric Paget Corps. was formed to undertake Massage.

Such undertakings as the Scottish Women's Hospitals and the Women's Hospital Corps, need special mention. The former was organised by the late Doctor Elsie Inglis, and was supported financially by the non-militant Suffrage Societies. The Hospitals were entirely equipped and

staffed by women, and by December 1914, £6,000 had been
subscribed. By the end of the war, no less than £400,000
was raised by women for the work of these Hospitals.

The two first Units were sent to France and
Serbia, the former at Calais, to cope with the typhoid
epidemic. The Abbey of Royaumont was taken over in
December 1914 and carried on till 1919. In 1917
another Hospital was opened at Villers Cotterets, which
worked till May 1918. Twenty-three members of the
Staff at Royaumont were decorated with the Croix de
Guerre in 1917. The Serbian Unit sailed in December
1914 and was stationed at Kraguievatz. This Unit
did magnificent work during the terrible
Retreat. Typhus broke out, and conditions were worse than
anything on the Western Front. Three of the staff of 50
women died of typhus - Sisters Jordan and Minshull and
Miss M. Neil Fraser. In 1915, a 3 rd Unit sailed for
Valjevo, and three Camps were also started. When the
hospitals had to be evacuated in November 1915, some of the
staff remained to stand by the wounded Serbs. The
retreat lasted for seven weeks, and tried the
endurance of men, women and beasts to the last degree.
23,000 Serbian boys died on that march, unable to stand
the cold and hunger. One Unit followed the remnants of a
nation to Corsica, where camps were opened for the
refugees. Dr. Inglis remained at Krushevatz, afterwards
being moved to Valjevo, where she and her staff were kept
prisoners in Austrian hands. One of the doctors wound
the British flag round her body, to preserve it from insult.
The Scottish Women equipped 2 Field Hospitals for service in
Russia and Roumania in 1916 while yet another Unit was
sent to Salonica. Dr. Inglis herself, after her release
went with the Russian Unit, until the evacuation of Galatz, when
the Unit moved to Reni, on the Danube. When the Russian
Revolution broke out in 1917, Dr. Inglis fought hard to save
the Serbian Division from being sent to "stiffen" the disorganised

Russians, but decided that, if they had to go, she
and her staff would stand by them. She was
by this time very ill, and she died two days
after reaching England, in November 1917. To carry
out her last wish, the London Units Committee
reorganised the Unit in 1918, for service in
Salonica, but they were moved to Sarajevo, where they
remained till 1919.

In addition to these activities, the Scottish
Women's Hospitals helped to rebuild the broken Serbian
nation in Corsica. Of the 15,000 Serbian boys
who were saved from the Retreat, only 7,000 lived to
reach Corsica. A Tuberculosis Hospital was opened for
the Serbs at Sallanches, and Transport Columns were
organised, to scour the country for wounded and
bring them in to the Hospitals. The record of
operations performed and of the 284,393 patients
treated is an amazing one.

A beautiful bronze bust of Dr. Inglis was done
by Mestrovitch, the famous Serbian sculptor, which is
now in the Scottish National Gallery. Dr. Inglis was
decorated with the Serbian Order of the White Eagle,
5th Class - the highest Order in Serbia, and given for the
first time to a woman. She also received the Order of
St. Sava, the Order of the White Eagle with Swords,
the St. George's Medal for Bravery under
Fire, and the Russian Medal for Meritorious Service,
1st. Class. Many of the other doctors were decorated
with French and Serbian medals for their bravery and
coolness under fire, and during the big Retreats.

Of the Staff, 14, Nurses and Orderlies, and
1 Chauffeur died on service. One of the nurses, Miss Fannin,
was drowned on the s.s. "Leinster", which was
torpedoed when she was on her way to Royaumont in
1918.

On August 12th 1914, Dr. Louisa Garrett Anderson
and Dr. Flora Murray called at the French Embassy in
London, and offered to raise and equip a surgical Unit
for service in France. Through the French Red Cross,
the offer was accepted at once, and the Unit was ready
to start by September 1st. So the Women's Hospital Corps
began its work in Paris, at the Hotel Claridge.
In November 1914, another Hospital was opened in
Wimereux, and was attached to the Military Hospital
in the Grand Hotel, and was definitely recognised by the War
Office, the women doctors acting as Army Surgeons for
the first time.
In the following spring, there was a shortage of doctors
in England, and, finding that a large Unit was
urgently needed in London, the hoppital in France
was closed, the old workhouse of St. Giles, Bloomsbury,
was taken over, and the Women's Hospital in Endell Street
began its career. Over 26,000 patients passed through
the wards including many Dominion troops.

One of the doctors, Doctor L. Woodcock, died in
1917, and five others, nurses or orderlies, also died
on service.

In 1916, 40 women doctors were asked for, to
replace men in Malta, and though no regular rank was given
them, the women went out in mufti, and did splendid work
in Malta, India, Egypt, Salonica, and in France, with
the Queen Mary's Army Auxiliary Corps. As time went on,
the women's services were more and more needed, and in 1917
one of the largest hospitals in Bombay was taken over and
staffed almost entirely by women. This was a great
success, and as a result, the American War Department
wrote, asking for information in regard to the
employment of women doctors.

The Endell St. Hospital was closed in 1919, and in
recognition of their services, six awards of the Order
of the British Empire were made to doctors, and eleven

Royal Red Crosses were given to the Matron and
Nursing Sisters. Members of the Corps who had served in
France received the 1914 Star, the British War Medal
and the Victory Medal.

The total number of fully trained nurses on the staff
of the Joint War Committee of the British Red Cross who
served in France and Belgium, Egypt, Russia and Siberia, Serbia
Montenegro, Roumania, Italy, Holland, Salonica, and on
Home Service, together with those given to the Queen
Alexandra's Imperial Military Nursing Service,
was 6,158. In 1914 the personnel of the Voluntary Aid
Detachments was 40,018, and that of the Order of St.
John of Jerusalem was 6,773. In 1918, these had
increased to 66,211 and 24,440 respectively.
The first V.A. Detachment, with two trained nurses,
started for France in October 1914, and formed a Rest Station at
Boulogne. In 24 hours, they had fed over 1000 wounded men.

Apart from the V.A.D's, the General Service Staff
(shorthand typists, clerks, motor drivers, dispensers,
laboratory and X-ray assistants, telephonists, cooks,
store-keepers, laundresses. waitresses etc.) grew to a
total of over 11,000. The first Convoy of 12 V.A.D
drivers took over a Men's Unit at Etretat in 1916; a second
and larger one went to Le Treport, and others went to
Trouville, St. Omer and Boulogne. A Red Cross Hut
for Interned British Prisoners was opened at Chateau
d'oex, in Switzerland, with 4 V.A.D's. These few
figures will give some slight idea of the many and varied
activities of the British Red Cross Society, though it is only
a small part of their work, and is given to show more
particularly the directions in which women were
employed. Some interesting figures follow, showing
the numbers of women decorated for special services
during the war:-

Nursing Members,	mentioned in Despatches	886
" "	decorated	329
General Services	members mentioned in Despatches	16
" "	decorated	1
Joint War Committee	Hospitals Members, mentioned in Despatches	103
" " "	decorated	34

In addition, 20 members received the 1914 Star, and 800 received the 1915 Star.

One hundred and twenty-eight Nursing members died on active service, and eleven of the General Service members, while over 100 other V.A.D's not directly under the Voluntary Aid Department, also laid down their lives.

At the Central Work Rooms, organised by the British Red Cross, 781,035 articles were made and distributed, such as sleeping suits, bandages, pyjamas, overalls, pillowcases, etc. The Home Workers also provided, through their various Depots all over the Country, 318,090 garments, and 220,499 surgical articles. Innumerable other Working Parties existed, which supplemented the work of the Red Cross, and no estimate can be made of the garments sent personally to fighting Units by individual workers.

The First Aid Nursing Yeomanry Corps (known as the "Fannys") did fine work with their Motor Ambulance Convoys. They worked from Etaples, Le Treport, Etretat, Deauville, Rouen and Havre, and convoyed the wounded to the base hospitals. This Corps worked first with the Belgian Army, but was attached to the British Red Cross in Calais in 1915. The total number of cases convoyed by all Ambulance Units was 7,233,536.

Women gave valuable help at the 10 Red Cross Hospitals opened in France, and in the many Recreation Huts which were started, each under a V.A.D Superintendent with members and men orderlies to help her. In East Africa, the nurses were hard pressed, for there was much sickness there, and in 1918, when the appalling outbreak of Spanish influenza occurred, the casualties in this zone were heavy. There

were V.A.D's helping the 15 Convalescent Homes in Egypt and
Palestine, and on all the various Fronts, including work
for the Interned in Holland.

The Prisoners of War Committee was under the care
of the Red Cross, and devoted and untiring service
was rendered through this body to try to alleviate
the hard conditions from which British prisoners
suffered in the German Camps. Masses of correspondence,
stores, parcels were dealt with, and but for this Committee's
assistance, many of the unfortunate prisoners would
undoubtedly have died.

Various more or less individual efforts were
undertaken, some of which are worthy of special mention.
Lady Dorothy Fielding's Ambulance, for example, did
magnificent work in bringing in the wounded under fire,
and for which she was decorated. "The Women of Pervyse",
too, worked night and day, bringing in the wounded before
and during the siege of Antwerp. Later, they started
a Dressing-station close to the firing line. In February
1915, they were decorated by His Majesty, King Albert,
and permanently attached to the 3rd. Division
of the Belgian Army. They were mentioned in Despatches
for saving life under fire.

Another Hospital organised and equipped by women was the
British Women's Hospital, at the "Star and Garter" Hotel, at
Richmond, for which over £100,000 was raised by women alone
for the permanently disabled men.

Last but by no means least in importance was St.
Dunstan's Hospital and Training School for the men blinded
in the war. The late Sir Arthur Pearson, himself
blind, opened this house for the purpose, and gave it devoted
service until his own death. The Hospital is still
at work, and has trained large numbers of blinded men in
various occupations, such as typewriting, massage, telephony,
boot-repairing, piano-tuning, and many other trades which have
made them self-supporting. Those who had the honour of

visiting this Hospital during the war, and helping in
any small way to lighten the terrible burden of
blindness for these men, invariably agreed that the
courageous cheerfulness of the patients was
an example to the whole nation. Many women were
engaged both in nursing and training the men. at
St. Dunstan's during and after the war, and the work
still goes on.

This brief survey of the work done by the
Nursing Services, and in allied spheres of action,
may give some slight picture of the immensity of the
field which had to be covered, and how adequately
it was dealt with, thanks to the magnificent response
of the women.

No record of the Nursing Services during the
Great War could be considered complete without a
reference to one of the outstanding figures of those years -
though she is chiefly remembered for something other
than her work as a nurse - Edith Cavell, executed
in Belgium by the Germans for assisting wounded
Belgian and British soldiers and keeping them in safe
hiding until they could either rejoin their units or
escape from the enemy zone. Edith Cavell was tried
and condemned to death, and perhaps no incident affected
public opinion more strongly than the story of how
she met her end. The words of her last message have passed
into the English language, because they are the simple utterance
of one who did what she believed to be right and paid the
price without complaint. She said:-

"I have no fear nor shrinking. I have seen death so
often that it is not strange or fearful, to me.
I thank God for this ten weeks' quiet before the
end. Life has always been hurried and full of
difficulty. This time of rest has been a great
mercy. They have all been very kind to me here.
But this I would say, standing as I do in
view of God and eternity, I realise that patriotism
is not enough. I must have no hatred or bitterness
towards anyone."

2. ESSENTIAL HOME SERVICES.

It is quite impossible in a short space to do
more than mention the innumerable directions in which the
women of Great Britain gave their services from 1914 to 1918.
New avenues opened up almost every day, and as more and
more men had to be released for the fighting line,
more and more women gladly came forward to take their
places. There was practically no industry, no trade,
no profession which was not invaded by the eager
volunteers, and bureaus, such as the National
Service Department and the Government Labour Exchanges,
were inundated with offers of help. In the essential
industries alone, by 1917 over one and quarter million
women were replacing men, apart from domestic service and
small shops and firms.

Early in 1915, it was apparent that drastic measures
would be needed to increase the supply of munitions, and a
new Ministry, to deal with and control this vital matter was
set up under Mr Lloyd George, afterwards Prime Minister.
His energy and driving power soon broke through the cords of
red tape, and shells, guns, aeroplanes and every kind of
ammunition were soon being produced at a rate which
would have semmed impossible in peace time.

As has been mentioned earlier, at the outbreak of war,
there were only three National Workshops in existence, but
these increased month by month, until/1918, there were 100, and
5,000 other establishments controlled by the Ministry
of Munitions. Between 800,000 and 1,000,000 women worked
in these establishments altogether, at every kind of process,
and exposed to every kind of danger. 220 Oxy-Acetylene
welders were trained and placed in one year; optical
appliances, lenses, surgical and medical necessities, X-ray
tubes - were all made by women, after comparatively short
courses of training. They handled high explosives in the
"danger buildings" for ten and a half hours at a shift; they

developed "T.N.T" poisoning, risking their lives and
health, to enable the men to carry on. Mr. Lloyd
George said of them:-

"We had some very dangerous work. It involved a special
alteration to one element of our shells. If we had
manufactured the whole thing anew, it would have
involved the loss of hundreds of thousands of
rounds of ammunition at a time when we could not afford
it. But the adaptation of the old element with a fuse
is a very dangerous operation, and there were several fatal
accidents. It was all amongst the women workers in the
munition factories; there was never a panic. They stuck to
their work. They knew the peril. They never ran away
from it."

Welfare work in connection with the women in
industry formed an important part of the organisation
in those days. Canteens and hostels had to be provided,
and Supervisors were appointed to see that the girls'
health was safeguarded as far as possible. The Young
Women's Christian Association did valuable work in this
direction, and, apart from other bodies, served over 80,000
meals a week in their Canteens.

Next in importance, from the national standpoint,
came the work of the Land Army. Within the first eighteen
months of the war, 300,000 agricultural labourers had
enlisted, and 258,300 women were enrolled in their stead.
Owing to the submarine menace, nothing more vitally
concerned Gt. Britain than her food supply, and, thanks
to the Navy and the Mercantile Marine Service, convoys of food
were regularly forthcoming, but it was absolutely essential
that the homesupplies should also be maintained, and
this was done, with the help of the women on the Land.
In Somerset, to preserve an industry, a special job of
Flax-pulling was undertaken by Corps of girls, with competent
gang-leaders. They were accommodated in empty country
houses, and the War Office provided bedding, while the
Y.W.C.A. undertook the catering. Some of the Corps worked in the
Army Remount Depots, doing stable work. Training Courses
were provided by the various Agricultural Colleges, and
outfit was provided. Girls were trained to drive the

motor tractors for ploughing, and later, the Board
of Trade organised women for measuring trees when
felled, calculating the amount of wood in the log, marking off
for sawing, and appointed forewomen to superintend
cross-cutting, felling small timber and coppice, and
all the lighter work of forestry. A number of
University-trained women worked in this Department
as measurers and checkers of timber, and others were
even trained sufficiently to fell quite big timber.
Early in 1918, there were as many as 2,000 workers in
the employment of the Timber Supply Department, of whom
1,400 were Timber Cutters. In Scotland, women were
employed on forestry work as early as 1916.

His Majesty King George employed many women in
his gardens and conservatories, and many
big estates grew special supplies of vegetables and
fruit for the hospitals and the Fleet, this work
being mainly done, including the packing and
distribution, by women.

Another aspect of the food problem was dealt with by
the National Food Reform Association, and the National
Food Economy League, both of which did active work,
instructing housewives in the scientific principles
of the economical use of food. Hay-box cooking was
introduced, and many other devices. Fats of all
kinds were saved, and in one year, enough waste fat was
saved to make glycerine for 18,000,000 shells.
Communal kitchens were established, with voluntary
helpers, and cheap, nourishing food was prepared and sold,
to save fuel.

Among the organisations which vastly increased their
activities during the war and did yeoman service was the
Young Men's Christian Association. This body enrolled
30,000 workers in Gt. Britain, and set up Canteens and
Hostels for the benefit of the fighting services on every
Front. From December 1914 to June 1920, 1,870 women

workers were helping in these Canteens, all of them
working voluntarily until the end of 1917, after which
time some of them had their expenses paid. They
worked at the Base Camps in France and Italy; they went,
in small parties, to Malta, Gibraltar, Egypt, India and
Mesopotamia; they did social work of every
kind in connection with the troops, they did educational
work - 150 teachers went out, holding classes for
the men - and they ran Hostels for the relatives of the
wounded, 16 in all, to enable them to visit their men in
Hospital, both at home and abroad. The huts run by the
Y.M.C.A were supplied with comforts of every kind -
books, games, clothing, cigarettes, soap etc. In
1918 arrangements were made for 60 wives to be sent
out to the officers and men interned in Holland, and the
Y.M.C.A opened and ran Hostels for them there. This work
was concluded in 1920. Probably one of the most
appreciated forms of help was the provision of free Buffets
at all the stations in London, where men returning from
the Front could get hot coffee etc., and were helped
on their way to their homes. No one who had experience of
working at one of these Buffets will easily forget
the sight of the men, mud-stained, weary, arriving from
the leave-trains, and their gratitude for the small
service which was rendered them at the Buffet. The
Y.M.C.A ran 1,000 Huts in Gt. Britain and 150 in
France, mainly staffed by women. Early in the
war years, Her Majesty, Queen Mary, appealed to the
women of England to join a Needlework Guild, to
be known by her name, to supplement the supplies of
clothing and surgical necessities made by the Hospital
Supplies Depots organised by the British Red Cross.
Branches were started all over the country, and in ten
months, 1,101,105 articles were received. A special
Committee was set up to co-ordinate the distribution of

these articles, to avoid any overlapping with other
sources of supply. Her Majesty's Guild still
continues its useful work, and now distributes garments to
women and children who are in special need. Queen Mary
also started a Special "Work for Women" Fund. At the
outbreak of war, many women were either in distress
through unemployment or because their incomes had
vanished, and this Fund was able to relieve immediate
need, until gradually all were absorbed into the war-time
industries which were set up. A National Register was
compiled, and the women rolled up in their thousands
to release men for the Army and Navy. Training
schemes were begun, to enable the women to be ready when the
opportunity arose for them to find work, and the Queen's Fund
helped to provide for them during the period of training.

Professions which were immediately affected by the war
were those concerned with music and the theatre, and
large numbers of singers and entertainers of every kind were
badly hit. As the many Camps and Huts grew in number,
performances were organised for the men, to cheer and
amuse them while training or on leave. Several Concert
Parties were organised which went out to France and
Belgium to entertain the men behind the lines.

One of the many strange innovations to which
Gt. Britain became accustomed was the introduction of
women working on the buses and trams. The London General
Omnibus Company engaged their first woman conductor
in February 1916. In all, 30,000 women applied for this
work and 4,603 were engaged. There was an age limit fixed
(between 21 and 35 years), and a strict medical examination
had to be passed, as none but the physically-fit could be
employed on this work. The women received a course of training
similar to that of men conductors, and others, after a
period of practical experience, were engaged as Instructresses.
Women Supervisors (many of them the wives of naval or

military officers) were engaged to look after the
women conductors, and a Supervisor was always present when a
conductor was interviewed in respect to mistakes she
might have made. Special accommodation was provided at the
garages, and rest rooms also. The women worked the same
hours as the men, and received the same rates of pay. Practically
every sphere of society was represented, and a large number of
the women had never been out at work before. Some were the
wives of the omnibus men who had enlisted, and many more
were relatives of the Omnibus Company's employees, while
others were the wives of officers on active service.
They all rendered useful and efficient service, and a
special feature of their work was the aptitude they showed for
the engineering side of the 'bus work, many of them
beingparticularly handy at all sorts of repairs. They
looked very neat and workmanlike in their blue serge uniforms,
relieved by white piping and silver buttons. During the air
raids on London, it was left to the driver and
conductor of the 'bus to decide whether they should keep the
vehicle in service or run it back to the garage. The
conduct of the women was admirable. When they did
show any anxiety, it was not for themselves, but for their
children or parents at home, and several of them were injured
by bombs during the air raids. Altogether, they did their job
well and tactfully, and were always cheerful, careful,
and considerate in looking after infirm passengers, especially
the wounded soldiers. They carried on until the latter
part of 1919, by which time most of the men had returned,
and on October 22nd 1919, the London General Omnibus Company
entertained the "demobbed" women at a farewell tea and
concert.

Of the special women's services begun during the
war, only one has survived it, as an organised and uniformed
force. That one is the Women Police. This arose out of the need
for a body of uniformed women to deal with the large numbers
of refugees who poured into London in August 1914. The late

Miss Damer Dawson, who was in charge of the Transport
Department which met the refugees at the London termini
and took them to the houses where hospitality was
provided, saw this need, in view of the crowds of
undesirables who flocked to the stations. · She promptly
applied for permission to organise a Corps of voluntary
women police, to act as patrols. Her success was at
once assured, and women of a peculiarly high type
immediately came forward to help her in this work. Almost
at the same time, another organisations was starting a
scheme of voluntary patrols for welfare work in areas where
military camps were being established, to act as friends
to the girls who were liable to frequent the camp areas.
This was regarded solely as a war-time measure, and had
no connection with the existing police force.
The Women's Police Volunteers were a trained body of professional
women, doing it as a whole-time job, and it was presumed that the
organisation should continue after the war, consequently Miss Damer
Dawson supported by the whole body of women involved, decided
on a scheme which would mean close and loyal co-operation
with their male colleagues. The word "volunteer" was
dropped, and the "Women's Police Service", came into being
early in 1915.

The reasons for the need for this service were
the dislocation of all the public services; the concentration
of raw recruits in training camps; the general atmosphere
of excitement; the presence of undesirable women and idle
girls and boys around the camps; and the liberal
separation allowances, which made many women better
off than they had been before, and which led to an
outburst of drunkenness. The Women Police were trained in
drill and ju jitsu, and in 1916, the Ministry of Munitions
entered into a formal agreement for the supply and control
of the force of policewomen in the munition areas, with
a distinctive uniform. They were first employed at Grantham.
then at Hull, an area seriously affected by air-raids,

Dr. Mary Murdoch, a woman doctor who did splendid service during
the raids, died of overstrain shortly after the
armistice. Many other towns followed suit, and at Gretna (near
Carlisle) where there was a large Munition Factory, a
special force was needed, to search the women
operatives (for hairpins, etc., which might cause danger);
patrol the danger area; control the canteen and pay office
queues; and, in the town itself, patrol and do ordinary
police duties. During the air raids, the operatives were
cleared from the factory, and the sheds and magazines
were left in sole charge of the firemen and policewomen,
and these women, guarding the magazines, took their lives
in their hands. Not one of them ever failed in her duty.
Ambulance work was also undertaken, as many of the
operatives suffered from the fumes of cordite.

Between April 1916 and December 1918, 2,085
applications were received, but only 1,044 were accepted
for training. 985 were supplied to Munition Factories.
Policewomen were also on duty at many of the Canteens,
such as the famous "Beaver" Hut in the Strand, London,
and continued their useful work during the
demobilisation period after the war.

At the Armistice, women were just about to be
trained for police work in France, but eventually, after a period
of difficulty, the Force was definitely recognised in
1919, and a limited number of policewomen were kept on, not only
in London, but in many of the large towns. In 1920, a
force of 50 trained women were sent to Ireland, during the
troublous time there, and in 1923 a further call came for
them, this time in Cologne, while the Army of Occupation
was stationed there. As a result, a small number of
educated German women were trained by the British police
women to work with them. Interest in the work had
existed in the United States of America for some time, and
in 1915, a well-known social worker there strongly advocated
the setting up of a force similar to the British one.

Policewomen are now employed in 300 cities in the
States, and in Canada, there are a few also working.
Two women are attached to the Police Force at
Geneva, and even as far as Buenos Ayres, women have been
employed as park-keepers, to work with the police.

The Women Police were employed altogether in
12 Munition Factories; 5 Filling Factories, and 10
Government controlled Establishments. At the time of
writing, there is a proposal to increase the numbers
at work in London.

Between 1914 and 1918, 198,000 women entered
the Government and Local Government offices, as clerks,
shorthand-typists, supervisors, welfare workers, and
interpreters. Many of them were highly educated women,
whose training fitted them more aptly for such work
than for occupations needing first-rate physique primarily.
They gave valuable service, worked very long hours
and released a large number of men for the Army and Navy.

Among the innumerable other organisations to
which the women devoted their energies were the Soldiers' and
Sailors' Families Association, a body created during the
South African War, and which administered grants from
the National Relief Fund, raised in 1914. The workers did
an immense amount of welfare work and visiting, and
started work-rooms and clubs for the women whose men were
away fighting, and later, for the men themselves.

In the early days of the war, one of the Women's
Organisations undertook the registering of Belgian and
Flemish Refugees, and found accommodation and clothing for
them, as well as providing 150 interpreters. Later on
it was taken over by the Government, which retained the
system of registration, and the services of the organiser
who had previously been in charge of the work. The Government
Employment Exchanges also, were supplemented by many Women's
Bureaus. One of these dealt with over 40,000 applicants for
work in the first months of the war, and the Government

Departments applied to this Bureau for their

Munition Supervisors, Superintendents of Woman's Staffs

in Government Departments, and so on.

On 22 other bodies set up to deal with War and

Post-War problems women were represented. They were

concerned with the work of the :-

Disabled Officers and Men
Food Enquiry Committee
Munitions Arbitrations Tribunal
Committee on Supply and Organisation of Women's Service in Canteens,
                    Hostels, Clubs etc.
Naval and Military War Pensions Statutory Committee.
Polish Victims Relief Fund
Serbian Relief Fund
Prisoners of War Help Committee
Reconstruction Committee
War Charities
National War Savings Committee

It can truly be said that there was no phrase

of the national life into which the women did not pour their

energy, thankful to be working hard both to help the men

at the Front, and to keep their minds from brooding on

the ever-present fear of personal loss. Those who lived

in London and other places threatened by the air-raids

suffered from nerve-racking anxiety for their children

and relatives and, as no men came out of the War as he went

into it, so no woman will ever quite recover from the terrible

strain of those days and nights, though there was no sign of

fear or panic shown at the time.

----

3. ENROLLED SERVICES.

Towards the end of 1914 and the beginning of 1915, various disciplined bodies of women were formed. The first of these was the Women's Voluntee Reserve, which, with the Women's Legion, organised about the same time, were to form the nucleus of the various Units raised to assist the Navy, the Army and the Air Force.

Another forerunner of the actual Service Corps was the Women's Reserve Ambulance, organised by the Green Cross Society, attached to the National Motor Volunteers, and this body had the distinction of being the first ambulance on the scene in the earliest serious Zeppelin Raid on London (September 1915). They came to where the first bombs fell, and when another ambulance arrived later, they were informed by the police that "the ladies had done the job." They also did most useful work in helping the War Hospital Supply Depots, and provided orderlies at the various Clubs and Hostels. Others met and transported the wounded from the Hospital trains, or took the men, on arrival, to the Y.M.C.A Huts.

All the women who joined these bodies were definitely enrolled for war service, and were drilled, disciplined, and worked voluntarily until they were more urgently needed in other directions.

Though the food supplied to the New Armies was good and plentiful, very few of the men knew how to cook, and the Cookery Section of the Women 's Legion was formed to meet the need. Many stories have been told of the round pegs in suqare holes in the Army, but none perhaps more poignant than that of the mathematical professor, a brilliant scholar, who joined up and was attached to a Balloon Section, and nearly poisoned the whole Unit with his cooking. As soon as the Section Commander discovered what an angel he was entertaining unawares,

he promptly removed the professor to another and more
suitable sphere of action. Organisations such as the
Women's Legion helped to remove such anomalies, and
proved most useful.

Later, in 1916, the man-power problem became acute,
and "combing out" was being vigorously pursued. It was
found that a good deal of work on lines of communication in
France could be done by women, and in 1917, the Army
Council constituted a body of women for such service. This
body was known as the Queen Mary's Army Auxiliary Corps
or more familiarly, as the "W.A.A.C.'s", and they were
enrolled for one year or the duration of the war, whichever was
the longer period, and they undertook to obey orders and serve
wherever required. Their principal duties ware cooking and
other domestic work; they also served as typists, clerks and
shorthand-writers; as storewomen, telephonists, and
telegraphists; as motor transport drivers; as bakers, making the
bread sent to the trenches; as gardeners in military cemeteries,
and they were accommodated in camps or houses near their work,
under women officers. Strict discipline was enforced, and they
were considered as part of His Majesty's Forces.

It was not until 1917 that units of the WAACS
were first posted in the United Kingdom. One contingent was
detailed for duty with the American Army in 1918. Altogether, about
10,000 officers and 52,000 other ranks passed through the
service, and 350 officers and 10,000
other ranks served overseas. As they were mostly behind the
lines, they rarely came under fire, but air raids were common,
especially during the Spring of 1918. It was at this time that
the only deaths due to enemy action occurred, and the Military
Medal was awarded in some cases, the tradition having been
established that, whatever happened, if the Camp were wrecked
every one reported for duty.

The WAAC's wore a khaki coat frock, with brown shoes,
soft hats, and great coats. Their pay was not high - just about as

mich as that of the ordinary private soldier, and the whole
organisation was officered and directed by women. The heads
were called "Chief Controllers" and "Assistant Chief
Controllers", and so on – they were not given military
titles, and did not hold commissions, but their
appointments were gazetted in the usual way. In England,
there is a very strong feeling that Naval and Military titles
should be strictly reserved.

      The Administrators (officers in charge of Units)
were trained in large numbers, as they had to learn to fill
up Army forms, make out pay sheets, requisition for rations,
cater and run hostels, and many other duties, such as acquiring
a knowledge of hygiene and sanitation. Usually, there
was one officer to every 50 women. All the girls were
usually put on their honour to respect their uniform, and
never do anything to bring it into disrepute. Many of
the Administrators though they had considerable disciplinary
powers, were rarely compelled to use them, as the girls grew
attached to them, and consequently would do more because they
liked their officers than because they were obliged to obey
them.

      Those girls who were drafted to France
in the grim, grey transports, were received by the women Draft
Receiving Officers, and went up the line to their billets, which
were in the base towns. Summer hotels, big houses, sometimes
a beautiful/Chateau, were commandeered to house the khaki-clad
girls. A great many of them lived in camps, in various kinds
of huts, with iron bedsteads and good blankets for covering.
One large Hut was used as the Mess Hut, and the food served
was the same as that served to the soldiers on lines of
communication –four-fifths of a fighting men's ration. The
WAACs were divided into 5 classes for work. Many of them served as
cooks and waitresses, and as many of them came from some of
the best private houses in England, the cooking was good.
In one camp, soon after the women were taken over, 60 men
cooks walked out and 60 women took their places. They were

more economical than the men, and, managed to effect savings
in fats and other essentials.

They learnt to do clerical work and send
requisitions for guns, trench mortars and every kind of
ammunition, and in some of the Departments, French girls
worked alongside of the WAACs. Some of the more highly-
educated ones - about a dozen of them - were known as the
"Hush WAACs", and they worked in the Censor's office,
decoding signalled and written messages in every modern language.
They helped in postal work, and handled nearly 3,000,000
letters and packets a day in France for the Army there.

One important piece of work on which many French women
were engaged, and on which the WAACs were afterwards put, was
the great "Salvage" work of the Army. At one ordnance base
alone, 30,000 pairs of boots were repaired in a week.
Old Helmets, leather equipment, haversacks, rifles, horse-shoes,
spurs, and every kind of debris of a battlefield, were
repaired and renewed whenever possible, to avoid waste.

Recreation Huts were provided for the women, as they
were for the men, and trained V.A.D's were attached to
the Units, to look after the health of the "Women's Army".
Serious cases were sent back to the Women's Hospital at Endell
St. in London, described in an earlier part of this article.

Another Section of the former Women's Legion - the
majority were absorbed into the WAACs - was ultimately attached to
the Army Service Corps, as a Motor Transport Section in 1916.
They enrolled for service in the United Kingdom, and about 8,700
drivers and motor-cyclists passed through the service. The
Women's Forage Corps, which included about 6,000 women enrolled
for duties in connection with forage under the War Office.

The Women's Royal Naval Service, known as the
"W.R.E.N.S" was formed in November 1917, to substitute women
for naval ranks and ratings ashore. Most of them served at the
various naval stations and did domestic and clerical work, though
some of the ratings were employed on cleaning torpedoes,
modelling, making mine-nets, gas masks, depth charges and sails.

A few of the officers were trained for decoding, and had to
deal with wireless messages, give convoys their routes, and
warn destroyers. A small number went abroad to Malta,
Gibraltar, Genoa and Ostend. About 600 officers and
6,300 ratings passed through this service.

When the Royal Air Force came into being in April
1918, the Women's Royal Air Force was also formed, being
known as the "W.R.A.F.S". Roughly two-thirds of the
personnel were employed on domestic and clerical duties.
There were some drivers, storewomen, and a certain
unumber of technical workers on aeroplanes and airships.
In 1919, 15 officers and 500 other ranks formed part of the
Air Force of Occupation in Germany, and in all, 566 officers
and over 31,000 other ranks passed through the service.

The total number of enrolled women, allowing for
transfers from one service to another, was close on 90,000.

Conditions among the WRENS and WRAFS were pretty
much the same, so far as administration was concerned, as
those prevailing among the WAACS, and the duties assigned to them
were similar to those allotted to their sisters in the Army.

So the women, after lending their help in every
essential industry at home, were finally taken inside the
organised forces of defence in the country, the last line of
usefulness and service. The women learned a great deal
from their war service, of whatever kind, and it did more
than release the energies of British women - it helped to
draw them nearer to their sisters in other lands, especially
those who went through the same terrible years of anxiety
and trial in the Allied Nations. They learned discipline and
loyalty to an ideal, and if it brought them much sorrow, it
brought them a wider freedom than they had ever known before,
and opened to them the gates of opportunity and service,
so that life will never be the same for women as it was before
1914, - certainly not for the generation which went through
and survived that ordeal by fire - and for the generations to come,
though they may not understand and appreciate the fact, that

freedom which was won for them was won by the unselfish

service and sacrifice of the women for whom the

Great War altered the whole face of the world and their

own lives.

N.B. Here follows a list supplied by the courtesy of the

Imperial War Graves Commission, detailing the

Names, Rank , and Unit of the women who died on

war service, together with the place of their burial.

By request the names of living women have been
excluded from this record.

Roll of Honour of British Trained Nurses serving under the
JOINT WAR COMMITTEE of the Order of St. John and the British
Red Cross Society who gave their lives in the War of 1914-1919.

Bain,	Annie Watson
Golding,	Bessie
McDonald,	L.K.M.
Montgomery,	Margaret E.
Whitehead,	Ida Kate.

Members of Voluntary Aid Detachments who lost their lives on
Active Service.

Abbey	Agnes
Acland-Hood	Miriam
Adamson	Annie
Adds	Florence Beatrice
Allen	Emma
Allom	Marjorie
Allwood	M.
Anderson	Margery
Armstrong	Sarah Jane
Arnold	Mary T.
Baily	Wilhelmina Mrs.
Ball	Catherine
Barker	Edith F.
Barlow	Florence, Mrs.
Baron	Margaret Alice
Barrett,	Violet
Barry	Anna Maud Irene
Barton	Mrs.
Bates	Madeline Elsie
Battersby	Mary
Beetham	Mrs.
Bennett	Hannah, Mrs.
Bennett	Kathleen, C.F.
Bennett	Olive L.
Bickersteth	Joan
Blackburn	Zinnia
Bousfield	Mary Cawston
Bowser	Thekla
Braithwaite	Margaret D.
Bramall	Ethel
Bramfitt	Margaret Elizabeth
Branford	Mary
Brent	Yvonne Rachel A.H.D.
Brewis	E.
Bridgeford	Mary
Briggs	Dorothy
Broster	Sister
Brown	E. Gladys
Brown	Winifred
Bruce	B.J.
Bryan-Daunt	Zoe Kathleen
Buckley	Florence
Bulmer	Rosa
Burgess	Meta

2.

Burtenshaw   Winifred Helen
Butler   K.B. Mrs.
Bytheway   Gertrude

Campion   Eleanor Louisa
Carew   Margaret
Carrick   Winifred Eliza
Carter   Ileene Meredith
Carter   Vera Lorance
Cass   Mary Elizabeth
Chadwick   Hilda F.
Chadwick   Mabel E.
Chapman   Marion Dorothy
Chinn   Lilian Ellen
Clements   Sarah
Clibbens   Beatrice L.
Coates   Winifred Stanley
Cook   Beatrice Mrs.
Coles   Daisy H.M.
Colton   Dorcas
Couldrey   Mary
Cox   Francis
Cousins   Isabella D.
Crewdson   Dorothea M.L.
Crichton   Dorothy
Crilly   Josephine Mary
Croneen   Barbara Mrs.
Curteis   Rosamund
Curtis   Amy, Mrs.

Dabner   Eleanor
Dacombe   Averill Mary
Dangerfield   Ivy
Dann   Maud
Davidson   Margaret
Davies   Eva
Dawson   Alice Mary
Denison   Florence
Dickson   Esther
Dickson   Mary C.
Dixon   Dorothy
Dodd   Emma, Mrs.
Dodd   Josephine
Dolan   Mary
Downs   Sybil B.
Dragge   Doris May
Dugan   Norah
Duncanson   Una
Dunning   Ethel
Dunningham   Adelaide
Durno   Margaret Isabella K.

Earle   Elspeth
Edwards   Marjory Eva May
Elger   Ciceley, Mrs.
Elliston   Evelyn Kate
Elwes   Emily Mary
English   Winifred
Evans   Margaret E.
Evans   Margaret M.

Faithful   Florence May
Fanning   Beris Burton
Farr   Mabel
Fawkes   Olive
Feeney   Mildred
Fenton   May, Mrs.
Ferguson   Monica Machin

Fitzgerald	Caroline
Flint	Doreen
Fox	Dorothy
Furlong	Winifred
Gailey	Laura Marian
Garforth	Stephanie
Gash	S.Mabel
Gawthorne	Lilian Richardson,Mrs.
Gay	Kate
Gem	Gertrude Mrs.
Giltman	Gertrude
Gleadow	Doris
Glover	Florence Gertrude
Goldson	Lilian
Gooch	Phyllis Mary
Goodliffe	Ada
Goodman	Dorothy
Gordon	Elizabeth Marjorie
Gordon-Jones	Grace
Gould	Emily Millicent
Grant	Elsie May
Gray	Mary B.
Griffiths	J.L.
Grundy	Marjorie Adeline
Guillemard	Phyllis
Gunton	Effie R.
Gurney	Sylvia
Hackett	Venice Clementine Henrietta
Haines	Jessie Maud
Hallam	Alice Violet
Halley	Muriel, Mrs
Hamilton	Lily
Handy	
Harding	Isabel Lois
Hartman	Emily
Harvey	Anstice Fairfax
Hasnip	Mary
Hasse	Margaret Helen
Heathcote	Marian Joyce
Hedges	Edith D.
Hellyer	Edythe Caroline
Hemingway	Bessie
Herbert	Julia Helen
Hill	Eleanor Frances
Hodge	D.
Hogg	Florence
Holder	Beatrice
Hollis	Kathleen Mary
Hood	Ada Annie
Hooper	Nina Louisa Mrs
Hope	Isabel
Hornsey	Sarah J.
Horrell	Dorothy May
Hutton	Eva
Imeson	Amy Elizabeth
Ingham	Daisy
Inglis	Annie
Ingram	Edith
Johnston	Annie
Jones	Ada
Jones	Dorothy May
Jones	Gladys
Jones	Lilian

4.

Jones	Martin, Mrs
Kentish	Edith Margaret
Kershaw	Annie
King	Dorothy
King	Nita Madeline
Kinnear	Katherine F.
Kirk	Jane Millar
Lambarde	Bridget Aurea
Langdale	Mary Agnes
Larner	Bertha
Lediard	Hermione Agneta
Lee	E.M.
Lee	Jeannie Smith
Leeper	Mildred
Lewis	Agnes
Liddell	Lillie
Llewellyn	Gwynedd Violet
Macan	E.
Maltby	Phyllis
Martin	Gertrude Mary
Matthews	Helena Mrs
Macintosh	Margaret Gillies Richmond
Marsh	Mary Alice
Mathias	Florence
Maunsell	Minnie
McCall	Kathleen Margaret
McDougall	Mrs
McGrigor	Louisa A.M.
McLaughlin	Maria Mary
Meadows	Phoebe Elizabeth
Meares	Ellen
Menelaws	Diana
Medwood	Lilian
Miller	Minnie Dorothea
Miller	Tryphosa Mary
Milles	Maud, Mrs
Moberley	Violet
Moorby	Hilda
Morgan	Hilda
Munro	Minnie
Murdoch	Alice
Murphy	Rosina Catherine
Neish	Annie
Noel	Mrs.
O'Donnell	Josephine
Ogg	Kate Elizabeth
Olphert	Florence Balfour
Orford	Eleanor Frances
Orme	Alice Mrs.
Owen	Meriel Georgina Bardley
Page	Doris
Paine	Phyllis
Parish	Maud, Mrs.
Parker	Lilian Lavinia
Parry	Ada Betty, Mrs.
Paulin	Anne
Pearce	L.N.
Peare	Hilda F.
Peel	Helen M.
Pen Pink	Margery Sylvia

Plumer	
Poole	Dorothy
Procter	Doris Jane
Quick	Lucy
Radford	Edith
Ransome	Enid Marian
Reid	M.
Richards	Ella
Rigby	Betsy Ann
Roberts	Alexandra Mary
Roberts	Kathleen Hugheston
Roberts	Harvey, Mrs
Rogers	Hermione Angela
Rolason	Mary
Rooke	Ellen Marjory
Roper	Olive Temple
Roskell	Gertrude L.
Roy	Louise Isabel
Row-Fogo	Gertrude
Runton	Gladys
Rutherford	Annie
Rylance	Olive
Samuelson	Leila, Lady
Saunders	Emily
Sellar	Olive Marianne
Settle	Florence J.
Seymour	Constance E.M.
Shaw	Ellen M. Havergal
Shaw	Lena
Shaw	Nancy
Shepherd	Winifred
Shimmin	Mona
Shorlt	Fanny
Smales	Florence Emily
Smith	Mabel E.
Smith	Mary Christian
Snelling	Gertrude
Snow	Edith Mrs.
Somerset	Alice
Sommerville	Janet A.
Spargo	Madeline, Mrs
Squire	Dorothy Jeannette
Stallard	Alice May
Stephenson	M. Sylvia
Stevens	Lilian, Mrs
Stewart	Christine
St. John	Esmee
Strange	Alice Marian
Sutcliffe	Zoe
Swan	Ethel, Mrs
Sym	Elsie
Tapsell	Kathleen Mary
Tate	Ethel
Taylor	Edith Elizabeth
Taylor	Ethel Lucy
Taylor	Gertrude
Taylor	Helen Batchelor, Mrs
Taylor	Nellie
Temple	E. Stella
Thompson	H. Dorothy M.
Thomson	Elizabeth
Thoren	Millicent Olive de Satge de
Thurlby	Lucy
Tichborne	Muriel Edith Forde

Tindall	Mary
Tonkin	Edith Mary
Tough	Helen Frances
Tozer	Mrs.
Trollope	Jessie.
Vaughan	Elsie May
Walker	**Jennie**
Walker	**Sara**
Wallace	Doris Mrs
Walladge	Hilda
Walsh	Sara
Warnock	Elizabeth
Warren	Florence
Watson	Helen
Watson	Hilda
Watson	Tamar
White	D.M.
White	Victoria C. Bazley
White-Jervis	Daphne Jervis
Wildash	**Henrietta Frances Bathurst**
Wilder	A.
Willey	Olive Jane
Williams	Irene
Williams	Jennie
Williamson	Mary, Mrs
Willis	Eliza Mrs
Wolfreys	Edith
Wright	Amelia Beatrice
Yeoman	Eva Dorothy
Young	Ada Elizabeth
Young	Margaret C.
Young	Mary Ann Eliza

Andrews	Ellen	Harkness	Bessie
Armstrong	Ellen	Hastings	Helen Munsie
Astell	Ethel Frances	Hawley	Florence
Bates	Frances Mary	Hawley	Nellie
Beaufoy	Kate	Henry	Charlotte Edith
Bennett	Helena Stewart	Hilling	Sophie
Beresford	Rebecca Rose	Hills	Maud Ellen
Berrie	Charlotte	Hobbes	Narrelle
Blacklock	Alice May	Hodgson	Eveline Mary
Blake	Edith	Hook	Florence M. Louisa
Blencowe	Mabel Edith	Howard	Florence Gwendoline
Bolger	Kathleen	Hughes	Gladys Corfield
Bond	Ella Maud	Irwin	Winifred Haviland
Brace	Frances Ethel	Jack	Christina
Brett	Norah Veronica	Jamieson	Jessie Smith
Brinton	Gertrude	Johnston	Margaret Hessie
Brown	Euphemia Lucy	Jones	Gertrude Eileen
Buckler	Elinor	Jones	Hilda Lilian
Buckler	Sarah Edith	Kemp	Christina M. Fuller
Callier	Ethel Fanny May	Kemp	Elise Margaret
Cammack	Edith Mary	Kendall	Rose Elizabeth
Challinor	Elizabeth Annie	Kynoch	Alison Grace
Chandler	Dorothy Maud	Lancaster	Alice Hilda
Climie	Agnes Murdoch	Lea	Hilda
Clough	Mary	Mann	Agnes Greig
Cole	Dorothy Helen	Macbeth	Margaret Ann
Cole	Emily Helen *a*	Macgill	Mary
Compton	Florence D'Oyley	Mackenzie	Isabella
Consterdine	Vivian Courteney	Mackinnon	Mary
Cooke	Ella Kate	McAllister	Clara
Cox	Annie	McCombie	Christian
Croysdale	Marjorie	McDonald	Elizabeth
Cruickshank	Isabella	McGibbon	Rosa
Dalton	Joan Glassfurd	McRobbie	Jessie Elizabeth
Danaher	Mary	Marley	Grace Margaret
Dawes	Emily	Marmion	Margaret
Dawson	Eveline Maud	Marnoch	Margaret Bella
Dewar	Margaret Smith	Mark Hannah Dunlop	
Doherty	Mary Agnes	Marshall	Mary Bertha
Donovan	Bridget	Mason	Fanny Marley
Duckers	Margaret Ellison	Meldrum	Isabel
Duncan	Isabella Lucy Mary	Miller Catherine	
Edgar	Elizabeth	Miller	Frances
Elliffe	Margaret	Milne	Helen
Elliott	Elizabeth	Milne	Mabel
Evans	Jane	Moreton	Ada
Farley	Martha	Murray	Mabel
Fearnley	Ethel	Nicol	Christina
Ferguson	Rachel	O'Brien	Moyra
Flintoff	Alice	O'Gorman	Eileen Mary
Forbes	Beatrice G. Frederica	Parker	Elsie K. Donaldson
Foyster	Ellen Lucy	Patterson	Jessie Jane
Garlick	Hilda	Pearse	Phyllis Ada
Garner	Annie Edith Curtis	Pepper	Edith Dorothy
Gaskell	Lily	Philips	Jessie Josephine
Gladstone	Elsie Mabel	Pilling	Doris
Gladhill	Annie	Radcliffe	Ethel Blundell
Goldsmith	Amy A. Victoria	Reid	Annie Campbell
Grant	May	Ritchie	Jessie
Gray	Emily	Roberts	Anne Louisa
Greatorex	Janet	Roberts	Jane
Griffin	Lillian	Roberts	Margaret Dorothy
Griffiths	Janet Lois	Robinette	Caroline
Grover	Alice Jane	Robinson	Elizabeth
Gurney	Elizabeth	Rodwell	Mary
Hall	Frances Mary	Rowlands	Helena May
Hamilton	Margaret		
Hannaford	Ida Durrant		

Russell	Alice Maud
Saxon	Ethel
Seymour	Constance Mary
Simpson	Edith
Simpson	Elizabeth
Smith	Frances Elizabeth
Smith	Jeanie Barclay
Smithies	Ettie Louisa
Spindler	Nellie
Stacey	Dorothy Louise
Stanley	Ada
Stephenson	Gertrude Annie
Stevens	Lottie Mabel
Stewart	Elizabeth Grace
Stewart	Wilma Bridges
Sturt	Kate Rosina
Swain	Lucy Melton
Teggin	Eugenie
Thomas	Lilian
Thomas	Margaret Evans
Thomson	Elizabeth Robertson
Thomson-Kerr	Mary
Tindall	Fanny
Townsend	Martha
Trevithan	Rita
Tulloch	Edith
Turton	Alice Mary
Vinter	Bertha
Wakefield	Jessie
Wallace	Elizabeth
Walshe	Mary Alice
Watson	Dorothy Mortimer
Watson	Elizabeth Harvey
Watson	Mary
Welford	Alice
Wheatley	Annie
Wills	Mary Elizabeth
Willison	Nellie
Wilson	Christina Murdoch
Wilson	Myrtle Elizabeth
Woodley	Ada
Wright	Hannah Elizabeth

O F F I C E R S.

Ainsworth	Grace G.
Beard	Eva G.
Chamberlain	Louisa
Edwards	Caroline M.
Elvens	Eliza M.
Grigson	Mabel E.
Prevost	Annette M.
Robins	Mary J.
Rowlatt	Olive K.
Wilson	Annie

) ------------ (

WOMEN'S ROYAL NAVAL SERVICE

O F F I C E R

Mackintosh	Evelyn M.

R A T I N G S

Beardsall	Elizabeth
Bowman	Hilda May
Care	Margaret Louise
Carr	Josephine
Clarke	Lucie Emma
Court	Helen Isabella
Davies	Caroline Jackson
Drysdale	Georgina
Drewry	Harriet Hawksworth
Duke	Charlotte Sophia
Elder	Mrs. Elizabeth Grant
Flannery	Mrs. Alice May
Hall	Mrs. Sarah Ann
Hunter	Bessie Sim
Hunter	Lucy Alexander
Knowles	Alice
Lockhart	Mabel
O'Keefe	Sarah
Pearson	Mabel Caroline
Readman	Lucy
Skinner	Phyllis Annie
White	Dorothy Maria
Wills	Mrs. Susan Sophia
Woodruff	Mary

WOMEN'S ROYAL AIR FORCE.

Aitken	Mary
Allen	Louisa
Ambrose	Blanche Agnes
Anderson Hastie	Janet
Anscombe	Daisy Maud
Armer	Alice Ruth
Ashley	Dora
Badcock	Dorothy
Blackburn	Elizabeth
Brignell	Alice
Broad	Netta Ellen
Chalmers	Margaret Hodge
Church	Rose Maria
Clarke	Ellen
Collins	Grace Zenobia
Conner	Annie
Coome	Agnes Hilda
Craik	Annie
Cross	Amelia
Daly	Alice
Davey	Violet Elizabeth
Davis	Marjorie Edsall
Day	Charlotte Annie
Dye	Mabel
Ellis	Florence Mary
Evans	Nellie
Fitzgerald	Marjorie Lilian
Gibson	Susan
Goodsell	Lily Seares
Goodwin	Barbara
Gray	Florence Annie
Harper	Lilian Florence
Harris	Lucy
Harris	Marianne Battelle
Hibberd	Ivy Petoria May
Holliday	Elizabeth
Horton	Amy
Hoxwell	Eunice
Hudson	Daisy
Hudson	Francis Louisa
Hughes	Ada Styles
Kennaird	Fanny Amelia
Lambert	Emmie
Lapish	Marian
Llewellyn-Jones	Frances Mary Dulcie
Looker	Nesta Mary
Mackenzie	Helen
Marsh	Lilian Maud
Martin	Ada Emmeline
McNeill	Catherine Marie
McTaggart	Jessie
Moore	Emily
Murrell	Evelyn Irene
Neal	Rose Edith
Nicholson	Mary Philips
Nutley	May Alexander
O'Donnell	Phylis Eileen
Payne	Marjorie Gertrude
Phillips	Ethel Alice
Piggett	Annie Louisa
Pigott	Alice
Plant	Lilian
Porter	Violet Maud
Purdy	Phyllis

Ramsden	Clara
Richards	Ethel
Roberts	Annie
Roberts	Elizabeth H. Jane
Roe	Annie
Scammell	Lily
Shaw	May Elizabeth
Sillitoe	Ada F. Victoria
Simmons	Annie
Smith	Annie Gertrude
Smith	Fanny
Smithers	Dorothy May
Sparkes	Florence
Spooner	Isabella Jane
Stanley	Mary Ann
Stokes	Emily
Taylor	Lilian A. Maria
Townsend	Florence
Tucker	Marjorie Annie
Turmaine	Rosa Jane
Walter	Gladys
Whatford	Nellie
Williams	Edith Olive
Wilson	Alice Francis
Woodcock	Margaret

WOMEN'S ROYAL AIR FORCE.

PARTICULARS OF 11 ADDITIONAL DECEASED WOMEN.

NUMBER	NAME		DATE OF DEATH
9700	BACKHURST	Kathleen Annie	21.11.18.
23146	CALDER	Mary Mitchell	1.11.18
5877	HOLMES	Lily Cecilia	4.11.18
574	LYALL	Annie	20. 2.18
12145	PARRATT	Beatrice Lucy	12.8. 19
11240	REEKS	Edith Jane	24.10.19
4316	SELBY	Lily	15. 2.19
17505	SISSENS	Lily	19.10.18
4206	STENNING	Annie	26.10.18
7834	VASS	Lily Florence	18.11.18
14937	WOOD	Annie Edith	15. 1.19

Absolom	Winifred E.	Ing	Elsie U.
Absden	Dorothy	Inglis	Kathleen
Bailey	Ethel M.	Irwin	Katie
Ball	C.C.	Johncock	Florence M.
Barford	Edith	Johns	Mildred M.
Barham	Ethel A.	Johnson	Minnie
Barrow	M.A.	Johnston	E.S.
Benoy	Florence E.	Jones	Annie E.
Billington	Sarah	Jordan	Lois
Blaikley	Mary M.	Knox	Jane
Bottoms	Louisa A. G.	Last	Julia
Bradley	Jane	Latham	Louisa
Brannigan	Nellie	Lee	Elsie May
Brewer	Kate S.A.	Lesser	Ada
Brown	Eleanor	Long	Violet A. L.
Brown	May Frances	Lord	Winifred J.
Bull	Mary	Luker	D.M.
Campbell	Beatrice	Lund	Minnie W.
Carpenter	Elsie V.	MacMahon	Agnes
Carroll	Kathleen	Maddocks	Dorothy B.
Cary	Bessie	Maddocks	Sarah E.
Cary	Hilda	Martin	Eleanor
Caswell	Margaret	Martin	Marjorie T.
Chambers	Mary M.	Massey	F.E.M.T.
Clarkson	Edith G.	Matthews	M.M.
Clitheroe	Mary	Maunder	Nellie M.
Cobb	Gladys H.	Mayers	May
Connor	Catherine	Mayne	Gertrude
Coombes	Violet G.	Miller	Annie C.
Cooper	Harriet	Mitchell	Francis H.
Corcoran	Annie	Moore	B.V.
Cotton	Rose	Moore	Sara M.
Crozier	Clara	Moores	Annie E.
Daly	Mary E.	Nattress	Edith A.
Davies	Madge	Nutley	Catherine
Davis	E.S.	O'Neill	N.T.
Daw	Winifred	O'Reilly	Marion
Dunne	Sheila	Page	B.A.
Dyer	Gertrude W.A.	Parker	Ethel F. M.
Ellis	Esther	Parnell	Elsie
Evans	Mary A.	Patrick	Lilian P.
Evans	Jane	Peake	Susan
Ferguson	Mary	Phillips	Violet
Foulkes	Elsie	Pickering	Edith
Franshaw	Agnes N.	Pooley	Beatrice
Galley	Amy C.	Petter	Ellen M.
Geoghegan	Bridget E.	Priestley	Elsie
Gerrard	Nellie	Quane	Doris
Gibson	Margaret A.C.	Rault	Nelly F.R.
Gooding	F.	Reed	Dorothy A.
Gosling	Clara	Reeves	Eliza J.
Grant	Jeannie M.	Richardson	Maud
Grant	Jessie	Roberts	Jean
Green	Ethel	Rodgers	Catherine H.
Hall	A.	Rogers	Marie L.
Hamer	Ellen Bella	Routledge	G.H.
Harding	Violet N.	Rowland	Mary M.
Harland	Eva M.	Russell	Eleanor
Harrick	M.K.	Saint	Lucy Jane
Harrington	Lena	Scholey	Annie E.
Harris	Sarah L.	Shayler	Nellie E.
Harrold	Helen C.	Simmons	Charlotte M.
Hodgson	Florence C.	Smith	Annie T.
Holborow	Rose M.	Smith	A.W.M.
Hooper	Katherine E.A.	Smith	Brunetta
Hope	Florence E.	Smith	Diana R.
Horner	Violet M.	Smith	Mary E.
Howell	Emma	Smyth	Mary
Hyde	Pattie	Sollis	Kathleen R.
		Speight	Louie

Spittle	Anne
Steele	W. M.
Stephens	Lizzie D.
Stiebel	Marie L.
Tait	E. E.
Tarr	Mabel
Thomas	Olive G.
Thomasson	Alice
Thomson	Ellen G.
Thornton	Dorothy M.
Todd	Barbara R.
Tooby	Frances
Twaddell	Maud E.
Twells	Alice
Walcroft	Kitty
Walker	Winifred L.
Wallace	Mary
Walsh	Betsy M.
Watson	Jeannie
Watt	Alicia
Weller	Ada. E.
Westwell	Mary
Whall	A.
Whitcombe	Amy L.
Whittaker	E.
Whitworth	Nellie
Wills	Beatrice L.
Wilson	Jemima
Wright	Elsie M.
Wright	Jennie
Wright	Maud
Wylie	May

MEDICAL WOMEN

Forster	Laura Dr.
Impey	Elsie Dr.
Lewis	Sybil, Leonie, Dr.
Ross	Elizabeth Dr.
Tate	Isobel Addu, Dr.
Wilson	Marion, Dr.

SCOTTISH WOMEN'S HOSPITALS

Inglis	Elsie Maud Dr (Founder)
Burt	Mary Ann De Burgh
Caton	Florence
Dunlop	Jessie H.L.
Earle	Agnes
Fannin	Teresa
Fraser	Madge Neill
Gray	Mary Sutherland Brown
Guy	Alice Annie
Jordan	Louisa
Leighton	Clara
McDowell	M.
Minshull	Augusta
Smith	Olive
Sutherland	Bessie G.
Toughill	Caroline Macdonell F.R. Mrs.
Underwood	Elsie Janet, Mrs.

Endell Street Military Hospital

Woodcock	Louisa	Dr.
Graham	Mary,	R.R.C.
Morrison	Gladys Evelyn	
Palmes	Joan Mary Georgina	
Prior	Eva Graham	
Wilkes	Helen	

AUXILIARY HOSPITALS

Addison	Clementina
Aked	Adelaide Beatrice
Allen	Alice, Mabel, Mrs
Ashworth	Octavie Leonie H.
Atkinson	Winifred E.D.
Ball	Clare
Baxter	M. Mrs
Beresford	Hilda
Birkett	Margaret Janson
Blake	Margaret Sewell
Booker	Ellen Mariana
Bostock	Ida M.
Bradshaw	Frances Maud Mary, Mrs
Bridge	Jessie
Broughton	Edith Delves, Mrs
Brown	Ledward Mrs
Buckeridge	Kathleen Mrs
Buckingham	M.A.
Butchart	Amy Kynoch
Carter	Edith Mary, Mrs
Cavell	Edith
Corfield	A.B.
Craggs	Olive
Cull	Dorothy Coleman
Deere	Kate
Digby	Elsie, Mrs
Ede	Dorothy
Edlin	Mary, Mrs
Evans	Katie
Falconer-Grant	Lydia William
Falkner	Marie Louise, Mrs
Fisher	Mabel, Mrs
Flower	Hannah Mary Parfitt
Gibson	Marjorie
Gilbert	Ada
Gillen	Gladys
Gordon	Agnes
Harding	Kathleen Mrs
Hetterley	Helen C.
Hodges	Constance Mary
Holden	Ruth
Homer	Hilda
Ingham	Sarah Louisa
Jaggard	Jessie B.
Jefferson	F.
Jenkins	Emily
John	Lisle
Johnson	Constance
Johnson	Gladys
Jowett	B. Mrs
Jackson	Dinah U. Milbourne
Klindworth	Florence

Lever	Beatrice Levy, Lady
Lewis	Flossie Hannah
Lloyd	Alys
Low	Isabella
Lye	Marjery
Lyon	Esme
MacNaughton	Sarah
Marchant	Ethel
Marsham	Constance
Martin	Ida
Mayne	Margaret
McNally	Clare Eleanor
Mew	Fanny
Mills	Rose Lydia, Mrs
Morgan	Jane
Morton	Helen
Paget	Isabella, Mrs
Palmeiri	Alice, Mrs
Pearson	Nelly, Mrs
Peck	Mary, Mrs
Penrose	Esme Keene
Peter	Mary
Pope	Helen
Preston	Elizabeth
Prideaux	Lily Jane
Rainsford	Frances E.
Redfern	Esther
Richardson	Gwen
Rhodes	Amy, Mrs
Roberts	Jennie
Robertson	A.S. Violet, Mrs.
Robinson	Mary, Mrs.
Saltmarshe	Myrtle Elnard
Senior	Mary, Mrs.
Shaw	Evelyn Fidgeon
Smith	Margaret
Smith	S.M.C.
Spindler	Nellie
Steell	Constance Muriel
Stevens	Charlotte
Stevens	E.A. Mrs.
Stevenson	Dorothy
Stirling	Lydia
Swinton	Ethel Mary
Thomas	Blanche Jane Barrow
Thompson	Minnie Bailey
Todd	Florence
Tough	Elizabeth Mrs
Tucker	Mary J.
Walford	Emma
Walls	Emma, Mrs
Whittington	Mary
Wilkins	Frances
Wilton	Mary
Wood	Margaret
Woollacott	Edith
Worledge	M.E.
Wright	Rose, Mrs.
Youle	Mildred

AUXILIARY HOSPITALS

Barnes	M.
Bell	G.
Bennett	Wilmott
Bird	L.E.
Boardman	M.
Care	M.L.
Chambers	R.
Clarkson	D.R.
Cox	F.
Crofton	N.
Crowther	L.
Croxton	N.
Denham	F.M.
Hall	M.A.
Harrison	W.M.
Harrower	A.
Hastie	J. Anderson
Hawkes	F.
Heritage	Audrey
Hodskinson	A.
Hollister	N.
Howell	E.
Hughes	E.
Humby	F.M.
Jackson	W.M.
Jinks	Mary
Johnson	A.M.
Kidd	E.
Lalor	W.M.
Lee	Beatrice
Lee	R.
Loram	Ruth
McKay	G.B.G.
Meikle	N.C.
Mitchell	A.M.R.
Newby	F.
Nodder	R.A.
Nowell	R.E.
Parratt	B.L.
Paterson	D.M.
Payne	M.G.
Pope	C.M. Legh Pickard R. Mrs
Porter	A.E.
Porter	V.M.
Rathmell	E. Reeves L.A.
Richards	E.
Russell	E.C. Robson E.M.
Ryle	M.C.
Salmon	L.
Salvator	Sister
Sinclair	C.
Smith-Sligo	W.M.G.
Smith	C.
Smith	Helen
Smyth	P.G.
Spiers	M.E.
Squires	E.
Thompson	M.
Titley	M.G.
Toran	M.
Williams	C.
Wilson	Ruth

BRITISH COMMITTEE OF THE FRENCH RED CROSS.

Cryan	Edith Maud
Davis	M.E.
Inman	D.M.
King	Grace
McDonald	Mina
Niven	J.C.
Pettit	Angele, Madame
Stevens	Beatrice

Surname	Name	Surname	Name
Abbott	Mrs.	Davies	Rosetta
Alderson	M.	Dawber	Mary
Allen	Mabel	Dawson	Emily
Allison	Mary	Deane	Agnes
Anderson	E.	Devonald	Esther
Armstrong	Mary	Dillon	Edith
Armstrong	Maud		
Atherley	Mrs.	Eady	Ciceley
Atkinson	Elsie M.	Eastide	Emily
		Eastment	Kathleen
Bainbridge	K.	Eaton	L.M.
Baker	Emily	Eccles	Margaret
Bamber	Diannah	Eddy	Leah
Barber	Mildred	Elliott	Lily
Barker	Maggie	Elliott	Mary E.
Barrett	Bridget	Ellis	Edith
Barron	Annie E.	Ellis	Lilian
Bashford	Nellie	Elston	Jane
Bates	Norah	England	Mrs.
Beckett	Helena		
Beech	Martha	Farmer	Annie
Bell	Annie	Farmer	Ethel
Benson	Annie	Farrar	Elizabeth
Benton	F.	Ferguson	Agnes
Blackamore	Jennie	Fettis	Hilda
Blackstone	Mary Jane	Few	Jane
Bland	Sarah E.	Fitzmaurice	Mary
Bolton	Grace	Flynn	Maggie
Botterill	A.	Foley	Mrs.
Booth	Polly	Fountain	Catherine
Bradly	Irene	Fox	Charlotte
Bradshaw	Margaret A.	Freeman	Annie
Brannon	Emily	Freer	Hannah
Bridget	Courcy	Frost	Annie
Brooks	Violet M.	Frost	Clara
Brown	Agnes (York)		
Brown	Agnes (Garston)	German	Margaret
Brown	Dorothy	Garrett	E.M.
Brown	E.	Gavin	Helen
Brown	Elizabeth	Gibbs	E. Lavinia
Bruce	Elsie	Gibson	Mary
Buckley	Gladys	Gibson	Mrs.
Bunce	M.	Gleave	Florence
Butterworth	Sarah	Gorrill	Ethel
		Grant	Eliza
Cameron	Margaret	Glassby	Ada
Carter	Florence K.		
Carter	Mary E.	Hainsworth	Violet
Carruthers	I.	Haley	Edith
Cashin	Bridget	Haverty	Marie
Cash	Elsie	Hawkins	Ethel
Chandler	Florrie	Hayden	Gladys
Chaplin	Louie	Heffernan	A.
Chapman	Katie	Henderson	Letitia
Clark	Nellie	Hall	Nellie
Clarke	E.C.	Herridge	Charlotte
Clarke	Fanny	Hill	Kate
Clippelier	Margaret	Hilton	Elsie
Clure	Mrs.	Hodgkins	Florence A.R.
Cole	A.	Hollinshead	Agnes
Cooper	Clara	Holmes	Annie
Cooper	Sarah	Horridge	Beatrice
Copham	Edith	Howington	Nora
Cotsford	Alice	Howles	E.H.
Crowder	Dolly	Hughes	Rose
Crossland	Mary	Huxley	Martha
Curry	Mrs.		
Cursley	Gertrude		
Curtis	Ada F.		

Jackson	Ethel	Schofield	Gertrude
Jenkins	Jane	Schofield	Mary
Jennings	Sarah A.	Scratcher	M.C.
Johnson	M.A.	Sedgwick	Emily
Jones	Lizzie	Seirs	Anne
Jones	Maggie	Shaw	M.
Jubb	Bridgett	Sheppard	Mary
Judd	Emily	Sheridan	Sarah
		Shoosmith	Elizabeth
Keenan	Annie	Silcock	Margaret
Kelly	Mary A.	Smart	Alice
Keyworth	M.	Smith	Annie N.
King	Mrs.	Smith	E.
Knight	G.	Smith	Ellen
		Smith	Sybil
Lazenby	Mary	Staniland	Stella
Leaver	Lily M.	Stewart	Amelia
Leonard	Ann	Street	Louisa
Levitt	Edith	Sykes	Edith
Lindley	Florence H.		
Ling	Dorothy	Taylor	Fanny
Lomas	Florence	Taylor	Mary
Lotinga	Marion C.	Taylor	S.
Lumley	Mrs.	Turner	Mary L.
Lyons	M.		
		Valentine	M.
Macey	E.	Venes	Lily
Marsh	W.B.		
Maskell	Mrs.	Walker	Jane E.
Mason	Elizabeth	Walker	Lizzie
MASSEY	Charlotte	Walsh	Elizabeth
McIntosh	Bertha	Ward	Eliza
Mead	Lottie	Watson	B.M.
Melville	Amy	Webb	Mrs.
Metcalf	Annie	Welsh	Agnes
Morgan	Margaret	West	Eliza
Morris	Lily	West	Mary
Morrison	A.G.	Whidgett	V.
Moulds	Nellie	Whiteley	Florence
		Williams	Alice
Newsome	Annie	Willis	Dorothy
		Wilshaw	Sarah
Oates	Elsie	Wilson	Agnes
Owen	Mary	Wood	Rose
		Worslop	Ida
Pannell	Mrs.	Wortley	May
Parragreen	E.J.	Wray	Florence M.
Payne	S.	Wyatt	Doris M.
Peaker	Sarah	Yeates	Olive
Perkins	Edith		
Perry	Annie		
Portman	Florence		
Post	Alice		
Power	Agnes		
Preece	Ellen		
Preston	Louisa		
Pritchard	Gladys		
Rainbow	E.		
Reid	Gertrude		
Roache	Edith F.		
Robertson	Bertha		
Robinson	Elsie		
Rodgers	E.		
Rofe	Alice		
Rosecoe	Margaret		
Rushton	Elizabeth Ethel		
Rowley	Mary E.		
Russell	Marian.		

MERCANTILE MARINE STEWARDESSES

Ambler	J.M.
Arnott	Sarah
Bruce	M.
Burton	W.
Campbell	A.G.
Carroll	A.M.
Cassels	Norah
Cochrane	E.B.
Coster	J.
Creeghan	Maggie
Dodwell	Eleanor
Duncan	Christina
Elbra	L.
England	F.J.
Fitzpatrick	Mary
Foulkes	Margaret
Hafkin	Sarah
Henry	Olivia
Hird	Agnes
Howdle	J.E.
Irnive	C.
Johnstone	J.
Jones	Mary E.
Kennedy	Eliza
Maberly	E.
McCormac	Margta
MacDonald	M.
McGregor	Agnes
McLean	Elizabeth
McMillam	Clara
Newton	E.
O'Callaghan	Annie
Oliphant	M.E.
Owen	Hannah
Palmer	A.
Parry	Louisa
Phelan	Elizabeth A.
Richardson	Annie
Roberts	A.
Robertson	Jean
Seymour	E.
Shead	Clara
Smith	A.E.
Stubbington	M.
Somerfield	Ann
Topp	S.
Trenerry	B.
Weir	M.

WOMEN'S LEGION MOTOR TRANSPORT

Butcher	R.E.
Cumming	C.M.
Embleton	F.
May	Rhoda
McMahon	A.G.
Watkinson	Rita, Mrs.

SERBIAN RELIEF FUND

Bury	Vivyan
Clark	Nellie
Dearmer	Mrs. Mabel
Ferris	Lorna
Marley	Mrs. Catherine Mary
Haverfield	Hon. Mrs. Evelina

FRIENDS' WAR VICTIMS RELIEF COMMITTEE

Powicke	Gertrude Mary
Henwood	Sarah

WOMEN'S EMERGENCY CANTEENS

Gartside-Tipping	Mrs.

YOUNG MEN'S CHRISTIAN ASSOCIATION

McArthur	Marguerite M.
Nisbet	E.M.
Pearton	Edith
Pickford	E.A.
Rowe	Edith F.
Stevenson	Betty

WOMEN'S LAND ARMY

Hammond	Mrs. F.A.
Nicholls	Mary Louise
Popplewell	Annie
Porter	Ellie
Gibbins	Maud Winter
Chapman	Mrs.
Davey	Lily
Garman	Blanche
Petter	Mrs.
Nutburn	Louisa

WOMEN'S FORAGE CORPS

Bettis	Edith
Bishop	May Victoria
Clarke	Daisy Kate
Coles	Gertrude
Gates	Eva
George	Bessie
Green	Ellen
Hancock	Clara Mildred
Howe	Annie
Johncock	Margaret Amelia
Kane	Lilian
Knight	Julia Winifred
Palmer	Ada
Smith	Ethel
Smith	Kathleen Mary Clayton
Whaley	Mary Ann
Williams	Elsie
Wiltshire	Elsie

MEMBERS OF THE NEW ZEALAND ARMY NURSING SERVICE.

Brown	Sister	Marion
Clark	"	Isabel
Cooke	"	Ella
Fox	"	Catherine
Gorman	"	Mary
Hawken	"	Ada
Hildyard	"	Nora
Isdell	"	Helena
Jamieson	"	Mabel
Lind	"	Lily
Rae	"	Mary
Rattray	"	Lorna
Rogers	"	Margaret
Tubman	"	Esther
Whishaw	"	Mabel
Speedy	Miss Louisa	Ellen

attached

Bennett	Wilmot
Folliott	Amy Charlotte Melora

MEMBERS OF THE AUSTRALIAN ARMY NURSING SERVICE.

AUSTRALIAN IMPERIAL FORCES.

Walker	R.R.C.	Matron	Jean Miles
Knox		Sister	Hilda Mary
Moorhouse		"	Edith Ann
Mowbray		"	Norma Violet
Munro		"	Gertrude Evelyn
Porter	R.R.C.	"	Kathleen Lawrence
Tyson		"	Fanny Isabel Catherine
Williams		"	Blodwyn
Bicknell		Staff Nurse	Louisa Nurse
Clare		" "	Emily
Dickinson		" "	Ruby
Hennessy		" "	May
Moreton		" "	Letitia Gladys
O'Grady		" "	Amy Vida
O'Kane		" "	Rosa
Power		" "	Kathleen
Ridgway		" "	Doris Alice
Rothery		" "	Elizabeth
Stafford		" "	Mary Florence
Thompson		" "	Ada Mildred
Watson		" "	Beatrice Middleton

AUSTRALIAN RED CROSS SOCIETY

Brennan	Adele
Grant	Lydia W.F.
McBryde	Natalie Mrs.
Riggall	L.B.

CANADIAN NURSING SISTERS WHO SERVED WITH THE

OVERSEAS MILITARY FORCES.

Matrons.

Jaggard	Jessie B.
Fraser	Margaret Marjory

Nursing Sisters.

Baker	Miriam Eastman
Baldwin	Dorothy Mary Yarwood
Bolton	Grace Errol
Campbell	Christina
Dagg	Ainslie St. Clair
Davis	Lena Aloa
Douglas	Carola Josephine
Dussault	Alexina
Follette	Minnie A.
Forneri	Agnes Florien
Fortescue	Margaret Jane
Gallaher	Minnie Katherine
Garbutt	Sarah Ellen
Green	Matilda Ethel
Hennan	Victoria Belle
Jenner	Lenna Mae
Kealy	Ida Lilian
King	Jessie Nelson
Lowe	Margaret
Mellett	Henrietta
Munro	M. Frances E.
Macdonald	Katherine Maud
MacKenzie	Clare
McDiarmid	Jessie Mabel
McIntosh	Rebecca
McKay	Evelyn Verrall
McKenzie	Mary Agnes
McLean	Rena
Macpherson	Agnes
Peel	Aileen Powers
Pringle	Eden Lyal
Ross	Ada J.
Sampson	Mae Belle
Sare	Gladys Irene
Sparks	Etta
Stamers	Anna Irene
Templeman	Jean
Tupper	Addie A.
Twist	Dorothy Pearson
Wake	Gladys Maud Mary
Whitely	Anna Elizabeth
Wood	Alice Armstrong, Mrs.

Dominion of Newfoundland

Bartlett	Bertha (of Brigus)

SOUTH AFRICAN MILITARY NURSING SERVICE.

Addison	Constance
Baker	Edith Agnes
Beaufort	Kaloolah
Bernstein	Dora
Black	Eleanor Eileen
Bolus	Dorothea Kathleen
Dunn	Gertrude Eliza
Edgar	E.
Edmeades	Constance Alexandria
Erskine	Marguerite Muriel E.
Firzhenry	Daisy Aletta
Hearns	Beatrice
Hockey	Olive
Munro	Annie Winifred
Paff	Pauline Hermione Emily
Wardle	Ida
Watkins	Julia Kathleen
Macdonald	Mina

Colonial Nursing Association.

Graham	Marion
Poulton	Maude
Winchester	Julia

Lightning Source UK Ltd.
Milton Keynes UK
UKOW03f0016041214

242521UK00009B/54/P